Age of dinosaurs. Dinosaurs are at their peak in size, variety and numbers and dominate every continent.

'K-T extinction'. End of the dinosaurs.

Mesozoic era

248 MYA – 65 MYA

Cretaceous period

144 MYA – 65 MYA

Hadrosaurus
Velociraptor
Protoceratops

Centrosaurus
Troodon
Tyrannosaurus
Triceratops
Ankylosaurus
Edmontosaurus

Giganotosaurus
Spinosaurus

Argentinosaurus
Nodosaurus

Deinonychus

Acrocanthosaurus

Iguanadon

Baryonyx

FULL TIMELINE

Oceans and atmosphere form. Earliest life forms in oceans.

Trilobites dominate seas. Still no land life.

Earliest land plants appear.

Insects flourish. First reptiles evolve. Shrubs, ferns and trees dominate land.

Massive volcanic eruptions cause mass extinctions, wiping out 90% of marine life and 70% of land life!

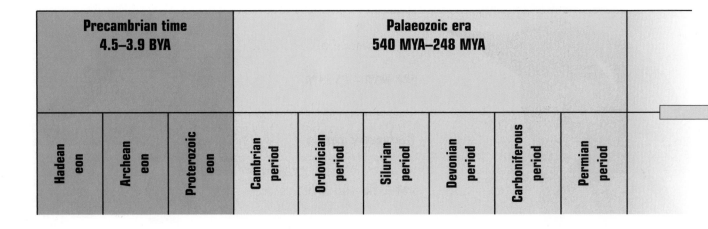

Precambrian time 4.5–3.9 BYA			Palaeozoic era 540 MYA–248 MYA					
Hadean eon	Archean eon	Proterozoic eon	Cambrian period	Ordovician period	Silurian period	Devonian period	Carboniferous period	Permian period

The Earth forms!

Sea plants begin photosynthesis.

First fish evolve.

Fish dominate oceans. Spiders and mites are first land creatures. First amphibians evolve. First forests form.

Synapsids, such as Dimetrodon and amphibians such as Eryops dominate land.

'K-T extinction'
End of the
dinosaurs.

Mammals such
as horses, bats
and whales
evolve.

'Great Ice Age'
Neanderthals and
Homo sapiens, or modern
humans, evolve.
Smilodon (saber-toothed
tiger), mastodons and
mammoths evolve.

Dinosaurs
dominate.
First mammals
evolve.

Most modern
birds and
mammals have
evolved.

Mesozoic era 248 MYA–65 MYA			Cenozoic era 65 MYA–NOW							
			Tertiary period (65 MYA – 1.8MYA)						Quaternary period (1.8MYA – NOW)	
Triassic period	Jurassic period	Cretaceous period	Paleocene epoch	Eocene epoch	Oligocene epoch	Miocene epoch	Pliocene epoch		Pleistocene epoch	Holocene epoch

Sauropsids
such as the
archosaurs
dominate.
First cynodonts
such as
Cynognathus
evolve.
Marine reptiles
evolve.

**Age of
dinosaurs.
Dinosaurs are
at their peak in
size, variety and
numbers and
dominate every
continent.**

Mammals
dominate.
Early carnivores
evolve.

Creodonts
evolve.
Modern
mammals
become
dominant.

Hominids, the
ape-like
ancestors of
humans evolve.
Thylacosmilus
and other early
saber-tooths
evolve.

Last ice
age ends.
Human
civilization
develops.

5

TYRANNOSAURUS REX

King of the tyrant lizards

FOSSIL FACTS
Fossils have been found in several places in the USA and also in Mongolia.

Powerful hind legs and very large feet would have enabled Tyrannosaurus Rex to walk and, probably even run for long distances in search of food. Even though its hands were tiny, they were armed with savage claws for ripping and tearing flesh from its prey. Its sharp teeth allowed it to rip flesh from a carcass and it could crush and grind the bones with its powerful jaw. It was also an opportunistic feeder and would also scavenge for dead animals whenever fresh food was in short supply.

Tyrannosaurus Rex was one of the biggest and most powerful dinosaurs. It was first discovered in 1902 and was named in 1905.

Tyrannosaurus Rex probably lived in family groups. Smaller dinosaurs would have been subjected to its fierce and often fatal attacks. Large Tyrannosaurus Rex bite marks have been identified in the fossils of other dinosaurs.

Dinosaur Data

PRONUNCIATION:	TIE-RAN-O-SAW-RUS REX
SUBORDER:	THERAPODA
FAMILY:	TYRANNOSAUROIDEA
DESCRIPTION:	LARGE, POWERFUL CARNIVORE
FEATURES:	DOMINANT PREDATOR

Permian period	Triassic period	Jurassic period	Cretaceous period
(290-248 million years ago)	(248-176 million years ago)	(176-130 million years ago)	(130-66 million years ago)

Appearance

Tyrannosaurus Rex was 15–20 ft tall and would have been able to see through the tops of the trees in the swampy forest it lived in.

The most recently discovered Tyrannosaurus Rex fossil was found in South Dakota in 1990; she's been called Sue after the woman who found her and is now on display in the Field Museum in Chicago.

MEGA FACTS

- Over 39 ft long from the nose to the end of tail.

- Could move at 10–30 mph.

- Powerful jaw of 58 serrated teeth each 6 in. long which re-grew when they were damaged.

- 200 bones in a full Tyrannosaurus skeleton – roughly the same number as a human.

- Fossil Sue was auctioned at Sotheby's for $7.6 million in 1997.

Dinosaur experts continue to search for new fossils and examine those already found to learn more about how this giant carnivore lived and died.

GIGANOTOSAURUS

Giant southern lizard (new king of the carnivores)

FOSSIL FACTS
Fossils have been found at various sites in Argentina (South America). The first was discovered by Ruben Carolini in Patagonia (Argentina) in 1994.

Giganotosaurus means 'Giant Southern Lizard'. It was given its name in 1995 by Coria and Salgado.

Giganotosaurus lived at the same time as enormous plant-eating dinosaurs like Argentinosaurus which it could hunt and eat. Like Tyrannosaurus Rex, which lived 30 million years later, it hunted in warm, swampy areas.

Appearance

Giganotosaurus was 18 ft high and measured up to 49 ft long but is not the largest dinosaur of all time; Argentinosaurus is the largest dinosaur at the moment and there may be more that we have not discovered yet. In 2006, scientists suggested that Gigantosaurus now been displaced as largest carnivore by Spinosaurus, based on a study of new finds.

Although larger than T-Rex, Giganotosaurus was more lightly built, and it is thought it could run quite fast. Its slender, pointed tail would have helped to balance it out as it ran, probably moving from side to side. It would also have helped Giganotosaurus make quick turns. From its skull, we know that it probably had a good sense of smell and excellent eyesight thanks to its large eyes.

Giganotosaurus walked on two legs, had a long slim tail, and had enormous jaws in its 6 ft skull.

Attacking prey

Those jaws were lined with serrated teeth, well adapted for slicing into flesh and up to 8 in. long.

Permian period	Triassic period	Jurassic period	Cretaceous period
(290-248 million years ago)	(248-176 million years ago)	(176-130 million years ago)	(130-66 million years ago)

It did not have the powerful crushing bite of T-Rex, and so would have attacked by slashing. It had three clawed fingers it could use to slash, or grasp with.

When hunting, it would probably have singled out dinosaurs that were young, or weak, or separated from the herd. Fossil evidence where several skeletons were found close together suggests that they may have hunted and lived in packs.

Giganotosaurs may have cooperated in tasks like hunting and protecting their young.

MEGA FACTS

- Weighed as much as 125 people.

- Appeared in 3-D in the IMAX® film *Dinosaurs*. Also in the *Walking with Dinosaurs* special *Land of Giants*, in which a pack of Giganotosaurs bring down an Argentinosaurus.

- The biggest Giganotosaurus was over 3 feet longer and a ton heavier than 'Sue', the largest known Tyrannosaurus Rex.

- May have hunted prey up to ten times its own size.

- Giganotosaurus had a skull the size of a bathtub, but its brain was only the size (and shape) of a banana.

Note This is not the same dinosaur as the African sauropod Gigantosaurus (different spelling) named by Seeley in 1869.

Dinosaur Data

PRONUNCIATION:	JIG-A-**NOT**-OH-**SAWR**-US
SUBORDER:	THERAPODA
FAMILY:	ALLOSAURIDAE
DESCRIPTION:	LARGE POWERFUL CARNIVORE
FEATURES:	DOMINANT PREDATOR

DEINONYCHUS

Cunning bipedal hunter

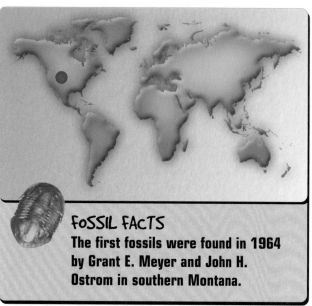

FOSSIL FACTS
The first fossils were found in 1964
by Grant E. Meyer and John H.
Ostrom in southern Montana.

The name Deinonychus means 'terrible claw' and comes from the Greek words *deinos* (terrible) and *onychus* (claw). The name was given by John Ostrom in 1969 because of the long, wickedly sharp claw found on the second toe of each of its feet.

Appearance

This carnivorous dinosaur was bipedal. It was about 4 ft tall, weighed about 176 lb and measured 10 ft from the tip of its nose to the end of its long, rigid tail. It had a large head with powerful jaws and sharp serrated teeth. Large eye sockets indicate it probably also had excellent eyesight.

Its feet were four-toed and it was the second toe that sported the vicious 5 in. long claw after which it was named. This claw could be held up out of the way while the creature was running, only snapping into position when needed for the attack. Deinonychus also had a pair of arms that ended in three-fingered hands with each finger having a curved claw that was long and sharp.

The long claw

Initially, it was thought that the long claw on its second toe was used to slash prey but recent tests have shown that it was actually more likely used as a stabbing weapon. Deinonychus' likely method of attack was to use its powerful back legs to leap into the air and land on its prey, kicking the long sickle toe-claws in, causing significant damage and anchoring it firmly. It would then tear and bite at the prey to cause as much blood loss as possible.

Its long tail was stiffened with bony rods along the spine. This tail would have acted like a counterweight, giving Deinonychus excellent balance and allowing it to make very fast turns as it chased down prey. We also strongly believe that Deinonychus hunted in packs, as several fossils of groups of Deinonychus have been found. Hunting in packs would have allowed Deinonychus to take on prey that would be too large for a single Deinonychus.

Brain size

The dromaeosauridae family all have quite large brains in comparison to their total body size, indicating that they were probably much more intelligent than other dinosaurs. This would have allowed them to work together as a team during the hunt and use simple tactics to guide their prey towards other members of the pack.

MEGA FACTS

- Fossil evidence shows Deinonychus packs hunted and killed Tenontosaurus, a dinosaur ten times their size.

- There is some evidence that Deinonychus may have had feathers.

Deinonychus

Dinosaur Data

PRONUNCIATION:	DYN-**ON**-IK-US
SUBORDER:	THEROPODA
FAMILY:	DROMAEOSAURIDAE
DESCRIPTION:	FAST, AGILE BIPEDAL PREDATOR
FEATURES:	SICKLE CLAW ON EACH FOOT, LARGE BRAINS, LONG RIGID TAIL
DIET:	CARNIVOROUS

COMPSOGNATHUS

Tiny, fleet-footed predator

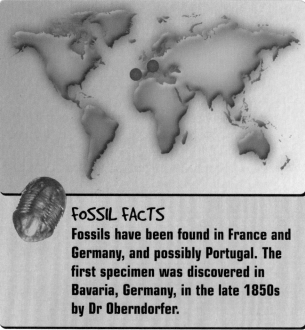

FOSSIL FACTS
Fossils have been found in France and Germany, and possibly Portugal. The first specimen was discovered in Bavaria, Germany, in the late 1850s by Dr Oberndorfer.

that Compsognathus was capable of rapid acceleration, high speed, flexibility, and quick reactions.

We know its size from two almost complete skeletons. Study of other partial skeletons gives a range of size from 28–56 in. It weighed only around 8 lb when fully-grown, and stood not much more than 1ft 6 in. tall.

Palaeontologists cannot agree over whether Compsognathus had two or three fingers on each hand. Either way, those slender fingers would have helped

Compsognathus means 'elegant jaw' and comes from the Greek words *kompos* (elegant) and *gnathos* (jaw). It was named for the delicate bones of its lightly-built skull. It was given this name in 1859, by Johann A. Wagner.

Compsognathus was an early member of a group of dinosaurs called the coelurosaurs ('hollow-tail lizards'). Later members of the coelurosaur group included the most likely ancestors of birds. Compsognathus had hollow bones throughout its body. This made it very light and fast.

Appearance

Compsognathus ran on its long, thin hind legs and had surprisingly short arms. It had a long tail to act as a counterbalance and to stabilize it during fast turns. Its head was small and pointed and it had a long, flexible neck. Its skull suggests it had good eyesight and was probably pretty intelligent. The characteristics of its skull and legs tell us

Permian period	Triassic period	Jurassic period	Cretaceous period
(290-248 million years ago)	(248-176 million years ago)	(176-130 million years ago)	(130-66 million years ago)

with grasping prey, which could then be swallowed whole or torn into pieces by tiny, sharp teeth.

Habitat

At the time Compsognathus lived, water covered much of what is now France and southern Germany. Compsognathus lived on islands in this sea. Although very small, it was probably the largest predator where it lived – the small islands did not have enough vegetation to support large herbivores, which in turn meant there was no tempting prey for large carnivores.

MEGA FACTS

- Compsognathus appeared in *Jurassic Park II* and *Jurassic Park III* as the vicious 'compys'. These films showed them hunting in packs, but in fact we have no idea whether they did this or not.

- Even fully grown, Compsognathus would weigh no more than a turkey.

- According to calculations made using the distance between fossilized footprints, Compsognathus could run at speeds up to 25 mph.

- The first fossil skeleton of this dinosaur that was found had the remains of a fast-running lizard called bavarisaurus in its stomach.

- In recent years the remains of even smaller dinosaurs have been found. These included the 18 in. long plant-eating Micropachycephalosaurus, which as well as being the smallest dinosaur in the world also has the longest name!

- Evidence of feathers has yet to be discovered on a Compsognathus fossil.

Dinosaur Data

PRONUNCIATION:	KOMP-SOG-**NAY**-THUS OR KOMP-SO-**NATH**-US
SUBORDER:	THEROPODA
FAMILY:	COMPSOGNATHIDAE
DESCRIPTION:	BIPEDAL CARNIVORE
FEATURES:	HOLLOW BONES
DIET:	SMALL ANIMALS

DROMAEOSAURUS

Swift and deadly bipedal hunter

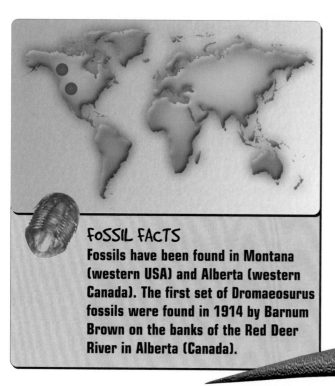

FOSSIL FACTS
Fossils have been found in Montana (western USA) and Alberta (western Canada). The first set of Dromaeosurus fossils were found in 1914 by Barnum Brown on the banks of the Red Deer River in Alberta (Canada).

It had a large head, containing a big brain – scientists believe it was one of the most intelligent of the dinosaurs. It also had excellent vision thanks to its large eyes, and probably a strong sense of smell and good hearing, making it an efficient hunter. Its jaws were long and strong, and contained long, razor-sharp teeth.

Attack

Dromaeosaurus' most dangerous weapons were its claws, which were sickle-shaped and on the end of each finger. Prey was probably gripped with the claws of the foot, while the

Dromaeosaurus means 'fast-running lizard'. It was given this name in 1922 by Barnum Brown and William Matthew. It is part of a group of dinosaurs known as dromaeosaurs, which are the dinosaurs believed to be most closely related to modern birds.

When first discovered, Dromaeosaurus was hard to classify. It wasn't until nearly 50 years after its discovery that Dromaeosaurus was formally classified into its own family.

Appearance

Dromaeosaurus was active and agile. It was about the size of a large dog, and balanced itself while running (and even standing on one leg so as to slash at prey with its clawed toes) with the help of its long, stiff tail.

The tail was stiffened by a lattice of bony rods and was flexible at the base so that it could be moved up and down.

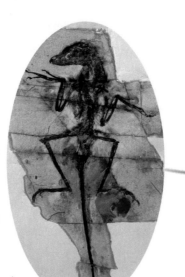

*Fossil of a juvenile
Sinonithosaurus*

*Skeleton of a
Dromaeosaurus*

MEGA FACTS

- Dromaeosaurus teeth have been found among the fossils of much larger dinosaurs, leading some scientists to suggest that they hunted in packs like wolves, so that they could bring down larger prey.

- With its deep, large jaw, short and massive skull, and big strong teeth, Dromaeosaurus closely resembles the much larger Tyrannosaurs.

- In 2001, a remarkable fossilized skeleton was loaned from China to the American Museum of Natural History. Scientists believe it to be that of a Dromaeosaurus — with feathers from head to foot!

- It ate small and medium-sized plant eaters like young Triceratops and baby duckbills.

- All 'raptors' (as dromaeosaurs came to be nicknamed) have the sickle-shaped killing claw on the hind feet — this was used for disemboweling prey.

finger claws slashed at the victim, though the sharp, hooked claw on each leg could certainly do some horrendous damage of its own. Dromaeosaurus probably hunted by running and leaping at its prey, enabling it to use all four limbs in the attack as it launched itself at the target.

Dinosaur Data

PRONUNCIATION:	**DROH**-MEE-OH-**SAWR**-US
SUBORDER:	THEROPODA
FAMILY:	DROMAEOSAURIDAE
DESCRIPTION:	ACTIVE, AGILE BIPEDAL HUNTER
FEATURES:	MASSIVE SLASHING CLAWS
DIET:	CARNIVORE, POSSIBLE SCAVENGER

VELOCIRAPTOR

Swift and vicious bipedal carnivore

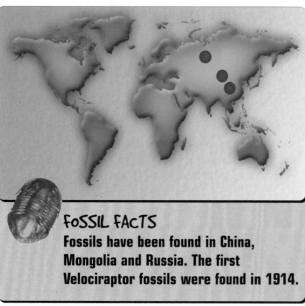

FOSSIL FACTS
Fossils have been found in China, Mongolia and Russia. The first Velociraptor fossils were found in 1914.

Velociraptor means 'speedy thief'. This carnivore lived in a desert-like environment around 70 million years ago, and may have hunted in packs, preying largely on herbivores like Hadrosaurus.

Appearance

It was about 5–6 ft, and stood on two legs. It had long arms and a long straight tail. Its strong jaws contained around 80 sharp bladed teeth – some of the teeth were over 1 in. long. It possessed large eyes, which gave it excellent vision even in the dark.

Velociraptor had an enlarged second toe with a vicious oversized claw attached to it. These sickle-like claws could be raised off the ground while running or walking, then used once the Velociraptor launched an attack.

Dinosaur Data

PRONUNCIATION:	VUH-**LOSS**-IH-**RAP**-TOR
SUBORDER:	THERAPODA
FAMILY:	DROMAESORIDAE
DESCRIPTION:	SMALL, SWIFT CARNIVORE
FEATURES:	VERY INTELLIGENT, BIPEDAL
DIET:	HUNTED AND POSSIBLY SCAVENGED

| Permian period (290-248 million years ago) | Triassic period (248-176 million years ago) | Jurassic period (176-130 million years ago) | Cretaceous period (130-66 million years ago) |

The claw experiments

In 2005 Dr Phil Manning performed experiments using a robotic claw designed to mimic the attack of a Velociraptor. The results showed that, against larger prey with tough skin, the claw would not have made wounds deep enough to kill quickly. The large claws were probably used to pierce and hold prey. Its razor-sharp teeth would then tear into the prey, causing as much blood loss as possible to vulnerable areas.

MEGA FACTS

• Recent scientific thinking is that Velociraptor was very close to being birdlike, and may well have been covered in primitive feathers for warmth and display.

• Scientists believe a Velociraptor could leap up to 12 ft to attack its prey.

• Velociraptor could run up to about 37 mph.

• They were probably warm-blooded in some degree.

• The Velociraptor had a very big brain compared to its body size, making it one of the most intelligent of the dinosaurs.

Breathing

Some scientists now believe raptors could have had a way of breathing like modern birds. Birds store extra air in air sacs inside their hollow bones as well as using their lungs – this means they can extract oxygen from air much more efficiently than mammals. A comparison between bird anatomy and fossilized dinosaur remains revealed many similarities.

Fossilised attack

An especially interesting fossil was discovered in 1971 in the Gobi Desert – it revealed a Velociraptor in mid-attack on a Protoceratops. The claws of the Velociraptor were buried in the body of the Protoceratops, its sickle claws close to where the jugular vein would have been – but the Protoceratops has the raptor's arm firmly in its jaws. Both seem to have died in a sudden sandstorm, or landslip, preserving their battle forever.

OVIRAPTOR PHILOCARATOPS

Odd-looking omnivorous raptor

MEAT EATERS

FOSSIL FACTS
Fossils have been found in Mongolia. The first fossils were found in the Gobi Desert in 1924.

Oviraptor philoceratops means 'egg thief, fond of horned dinosaurs'.

Oviraptor was a small, fast-moving biped with long slender legs and short arms for grasping. At the ends of these arms were large three-fingered hands with claws up to 3 in. long. It had a flexible neck, a long tail, its powerful jaws were designed for crushing and its skull was almost parrot-shaped. On top of its snout was a thin bony crest, which seemed to change with age.

The shape of Oviraptor's head and mouth would have made it equipped for dealing with a variety of food. It was probably an omnivore, making up its diet from almost anything it could find – for example, meat, plants, eggs, insects and shellfish. Omnivorous dinosaurs are very rare.

Permian period	Triassic period	Jurassic period	Cretaceous period
(290-248 million years ago)	(248-176 million years ago)	(176-130 million years ago)	(130-66 million years ago)

Fossil

MEGA FACTS

- Oviraptor could run at about 43 mph.

- It was 6–8 ft long and weighed about 80 lb.

- If an Oviraptor sat on its eggs to keep them warm, that would mean it was warm-blooded. However, they may have sat on their eggs for other reasons, like protecting them.

- Its crest may have been used for mating display, or to distinguish between males and females.

- Oviraptors share many characteristics with birds, and may have been covered in feathers.

Wrongly accused

The original fossil find was misinterpreted by the scientists that studied it. They found the fossil of the Oviraptor near a nest containing dinosaur eggs – these eggs were assumed to belong to another dinosaur. The scientists thought the Ovirapor must have been stealing the eggs for food and so gave it its name of 'egg thief'.

In 1993 a team of American and Mongolian scientists found a fossil of an egg of the same kind – and this time found an Oviraptor embryo inside it. It seemed that the Oviraptor found in 1924 had been protecting its own nest!

Further evidence of the Oviraptor's 'nurturing' nature came with the discovery in 1995 of a fossil Oviraptor actually sitting on its nest. The Oviraptor had its feet folded underneath its body, and a clutch of at least 15 eggs were arranged in a circle and surrounded by its forearms.

Reproduction

A recent discovery from Jiangxi in China showed a partial skeleton of an Oviraptor who was about to give birth, with intact eggs with shells still inside the body. Examination of the find showed that the reproductive system of an Oviraptor is something between that of reptiles and birds, having similarities to each. This is taken as further evidence of the theory that birds evolved from dinosaurs.

Dinosaur Data

PRONUNCIATION:	O-VIH-**RAP**-TOR
SUBORDER:	THERAPODA
FAMILY:	OVIRAPTORIDAE
DESCRIPTION:	BIPEDAL OMNIVORE
FEATURES:	TOOTHLESS BEAK, HORNY CREST IN TOP OF HEAD
DIET:	OMNIVOROUS

ACROCANTHOSAURUS

Gigantic bipedal hunter

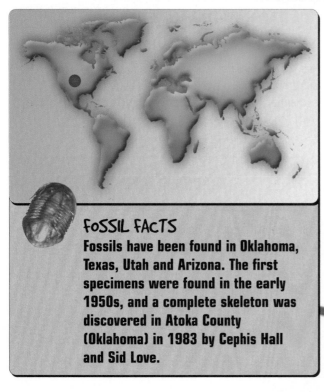

Acrocanthosaurus means 'high-spined lizard'. It gets this name from the unusual spikes which grew out of its spine.

Appearance

'Acro' (as the dinosaur is often nicknamed) was 42 ft in length and weighed 5,000 lb. Acro's teeth were designed for tearing meat from the bones of its prey, not for crushing and cracking.

Acro was a meat eater, and had a skull very similar to that of Allosaurus. It had typical Allosaur 'eye horns', developed into ridges to protect the eyes –

a second ridge ran along the top of the nose and joined up with the eye ridges. The unusually deep back part of its lower jaw gave it a very powerful bite. Its hands were nothing like an Allosaur's, however – it had three-fingered hands equipped with sickle-shaped claws, shaped for holding prey rather than puncturing skin.

The spines

The tall spines on the backbone of Acrocanthosaurus ran from its neck down to the front half of its tail.

FOSSIL FACTS

Fossils have been found in Oklahoma, Texas, Utah and Arizona. The first specimens were found in the early 1950s, and a complete skeleton was discovered in Atoka County (Oklahoma) in 1983 by Cephis Hall and Sid Love.

Scientists originally thought this must mean it had a 'sail' on its back like Dimetrodon. More recent thinking is that it had more of a 'hump-backed' shape than a sail, but the exact purpose of the spines is still a mystery.

They may have been anchors for powerful muscles. If so, it would mean Acro was very strong indeed – and it would have needed to be to catch the huge sauropod dinosaurs its fossilized footprints show it tracking! Some modern animals, for example, elephants, horses and buffalo, have this kind of muscle suspension.

The spines might also have been used to communicate with other Acros, and to regulate body temperature. They would have provided Acro with extra surface area, which would be helpful for both the display of colour and pattern, and for absorbing and getting rid of heat. This would have been very useful in the tropical climate in which it lived.

Dinosaur Data

PRONUNCIATION:	AK-ROW-**KAN**-THO-**SAWR**-US
SUBORDER:	THERAPODA
DESCRIPTION:	LARGE, POWERFUL MEAT EATER
FEATURES:	TALL RIDGE SPINES
DIET:	CARNIVORE AND POSSIBLY SCAVENGER

MEGA FACTS

- This dinosaur would probably be able to lift a small car off the ground if it were alive today. Its arms were larger and more powerful than those of T-Rex itself.

- Acrocanthosaurus appeared in the multi-platform video game *Jurassic Park: Operation Genesis*. It is shown catching a Dryosaurus for dinner.

- In 2005, scientists constructed a replica of Acro's brain, using CT scanning technology on a fossil skull. The result showed that the brain was more like that of a crocodile than a bird in shape, that Acro probably had excellent hearing, and that its head would have been held at an angle 25 degrees beneath horizontal.

- As any of its 68 serrated teeth broke, another was ready to take its place. Like a shark, Acro was constantly shedding old teeth and replacing them with new ones.

- In 1998, the fossil skeleton of an Acrocanthosaurus nicknamed 'Fran' was bought for the North Carolina Museum of Natural Sciences for $3 million, believed to be the second highest price ever paid for a dinosaur.

ALLOSAURUS

Dominant flesh eater

MEAT EATERS

legs and very powerful arms. It also had large claws on its hands – one claw discovered was more than 11 ft long.

Allosaurus was light thanks to air sacs in its bones – this would have allowed it to run very fast, and also to leap at its prey, tear out a chunk with its teeth and then leap away again.

FOSSIL FACTS
Fossils have been found in the Western USA and (recently) in Europe. The first fossils were found in Colarado.

Allosaurus means 'different lizard', so named because its vertebrae (backbones) were different from those of all other dinosaurs. The first specimen was studied and named by Othniel C. March in 1877.

Appearance

Allosaurus was between 23–39 ft in length, 10–15 ft tall and weighed 1–4 tons. It had a huge head, long strong hind

Dinosaur Data

PRONUNCIATION:	AL-UH-**SAWR**-US
SUBORDER:	THERAPODA
FAMILY:	ALLOSAURIDAE
DESCRIPTION:	BIPEDAL CARNIVORE
FEATURES:	HINGED JAW, BLUNT HORNS
DIET:	PLANT-EATING DINOSAURS

Allosaurus was the most common large predator in North America 155–145 million years ago – so many fossil remains have been found in this area that some scientists suggest Allosaurus might have hunted in large packs.

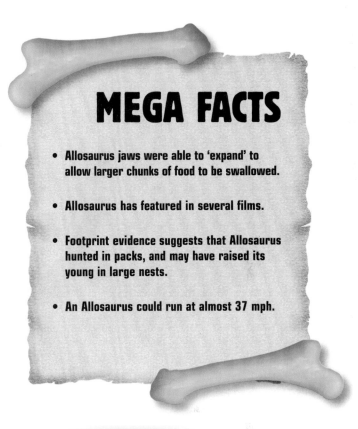

Skeletons

In 1991, a 95% complete skeleton of a young Allosaurus was discovered and named 'Big Al'. Big Al was 26 ft in length and 19 of his bones showed signs of breakage or infection. He was discovered by a Swiss team led by Kirby Siber. The same team later excavated an even more impressive Allosaurus skeleton – the best preserved of its kind to date – which was promptly christened 'Big Al 2'.

Attacking prey

Recently, more information has come to light about the way an Allosaurus attacked its prey. A scientist at Cambridge University (England) called Emily Rayfield created a computer model of Big Al's skull, using techniques usually used in engineering.

The model allowed her to calculate the force that Big Al's jaws would have needed to break the skull of a living creature. She concluded that Allosaurus actually had quite a weak bite.

The skull was also very light, but capable of withstanding massive upwards force. Rayfield concluded that the Allosaur had actually attacked by opening its mouth wide and using powerful neck muscles to drive its upper jaw downward, slamming into its prey like an axe and tearing away hunks of flesh.

MEGA FACTS

- Allosaurus jaws were able to 'expand' to allow larger chunks of food to be swallowed.

- Allosaurus has featured in several films.

- Footprint evidence suggests that Allosaurus hunted in packs, and may have raised its young in large nests.

- An Allosaurus could run at almost 37 mph.

SAURORNITHOIDES

Big-brained bird-like carnivore

Saurornithoides means 'bird-like lizard'. It was named in 1924 by Osborn and comes from the Greek stems *saur* (lizard) *ornitho* (bird) and *oid* (form).

Like other members of its family, Saurornithoides was a highly-efficient predator. It had a long, low head and sharp, closely-packed teeth. Like other raptors, it ran on its strong hind legs and probably used its long arms and grasping hands to seize and tear at live prey, including small mammals and possibly other dinosaur hatchlings.

It had one especially long, vicious claw on its hind feet, which was attached to the fourth toe, and was retractable when running or walking.

Much of what we know about this dinosaur comes from fossilized skull material – no complete skeleton has been found anywhere.

Dinosaur Data

PRONUNCIATION:	**SAWR**-OR-NIH-**THOY**-DEEZ
SUBORDER:	THERAPODA
FAMILY:	TROODONTIDAE
DESCRIPTION:	BIRD-LIKE BIPEDAL CARNIVORE
FEATURES:	HUGE RETRACTABLE CLAW, BIG BRAIN
DIET:	SMALLER MAMMALS, INSECTS

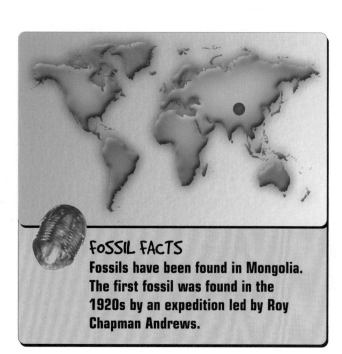

FOSSIL FACTS
Fossils have been found in Mongolia. The first fossil was found in the 1920s by an expedition led by Roy Chapman Andrews.

Skulls

The skull fossils show that Saurornithoides had a very large brain compared to the size of its body, making it one of the most intelligent of the dinosaurs. Its brain was six times as big as that of a crocodile.

The skulls also show that this dinosaur had large eyes, positioned forward so as to give it binocular vision. This would have been a big help while hunting – for example, allowing Saurornithoides to accurately judge distances. Most dinosaurs had eyes on the sides of their heads. It probably also had excellent night vision, and may even have been primarily nocturnal.

When the first Saurornithoides fossils were discovered, its long, narrow snout tricked those studying it into thinking it was actually an ancient bird. There is still debate as to just how like a bird the 'lizard bird form' really was. Many scientists, for example, now believe its body may have been covered in feathers. Further study (and, hopefully, new discoveries) will be needed before the secrets of this smart little dinosaur are revealed.

MEGA FACTS

- Estimated to be 6–10 ft in length.

- Weighed about 29–59 lb.

- Fossils from very similar dinosaurs have been found in North America, suggesting that 85–77 million years ago, the climates of Mongolia and North America were similar.

- It was a smart dinosaur as it had the biggest brain relative to its body size of any of the dinosaurs.

- It was also sharp-eyed, as it had large eyes and binocular vision.

CARNOTAURUS

Horned gigantic carnivore

FOSSIL FACTS
The first (and only) fossil of the Carnotaurus was found in Patagonia (South America) in 1985 by José F. Bonaparte.

Carnotaurus grew to about 25 ft long and stood about 15 ft tall on its hind legs. It moved on two feet and had a long thin tail. We do not know if it had the speed and agility to hunt down prey, but its short, pointed teeth show us it was a meat eater. Instead of hunting, it may have scavenged from the bodies of dead animals.

It had unusually small arms for a therapod (probably the tiniest of any meat eater), and its hands had four fingers (one finger being a spike that was directed backwards). These fingers had sharp claws, which it used to hold and tear at its food. The Carnotaurus' hands do not bend and, strangely, seem to be attached directly to its body.

Skull

The skull of Carnotaurus measures only 9 in., showing it had a much shorter snout that other therapods. Its eyes were set facing slightly forwards, so unlike most dinosaurs it may have had partial binocular vision (the ability to focus on one object with both eyes, which is very useful for judging distance).

Carnotaurus means 'meat-eating bull'. It was named in 1985 by José F. Bonaparte. It is named from its most notable feature – the two horns located above its eyes, resembling those of a bull. The name comes from the Greek words *carn* (flesh) and *taurus* (bull).

The purpose of these horns is not known. It is possible that they were used for display – for attracting mates, or showing dominance.

This enormous dinosaur lived about 113–91 million years ago in what is now Argentina. It had a small skull, a broad chest and a thin tail.

Appearance

Everything we know about Carnotaurus comes from one find, an almost complete skeleton. The skeleton was so well-preserved, it even kept impressions of the Carnotaurus' rough, bumpy skin all down its right hand side.

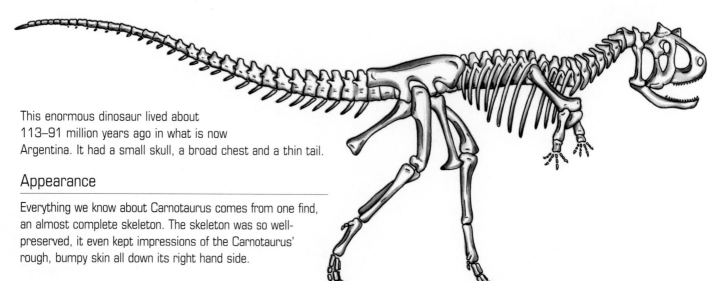

Carnotaurus skeleton

MEGA FACTS

- A piece of fossilized skin from the head of a Carnotaurus shows a pattern of small scales, with larger scales covering prominent positions like the snout. These larger scales may have made these areas more colourful, as is quite common in lizards.

- More than five times as big as an African lion.

- Carnotaurus was one of the major villains in Disney's animated film *Dinosaur*.

- Carnotaurus weighed about 1 ton.

- Carnotaurus featured in the Michael Crichton novel *The Lost World*, but didn't make it into the film version – the film-makers opted for a Ceratosaurus instead.

Dinosaur Data

PRONUNCIATION:	KAR-NO-TAWR-US
SUBORDER:	THERAPODA
FAMILY:	ABELISAURIDAE
DESCRIPTION:	HORNED CARNIVORE
FEATURES:	EYEHORNS, TINY ARMS
DIET:	OTHER DINOSAURS, MAY HAVE SCAVENGED ON DEAD BODIES

27

TROODON

Intelligent bipedal dinosaur

MEAT EATERS

FOSSIL FACTS
The first fossil was found by Ferdinand V. Hayden in 1855. Fossils have been found in the USA and Canada.

Appearance

Troodon was a biped with long hind legs, relatively short arms, a long thin jaw with sharp serrated teeth and a stiff tail that would have helped it balance when running and leaping.

It weighed about 175 lb. It was about 12 ft long and 3 ft tall at the hips.

Its long hind legs had large, sickle-shaped claws on the second toes of each foot. Troodon used these claws for kicking into its prey, to cause terrible wounds and prevent it being thrown off as it used its teeth and front claws to bite and tear. The sickle claws were much longer than the other toes' claws and would have been kept

Troodon was discovered by Ferdinand Hayden in 1855 and named by Joseph Leidy in 1856. The name means 'wounding tooth'. It was named after the serrated tooth that was the first fragment of its skeleton to be found.

Troodon tooth

Dinosaur Data

PRONUNCIATION:	**TRUE**-OH-DON
SUBORDER:	THEROPODA
FAMILY:	TROODONTIDAE
DESCRIPTION:	LARGE-EYED INTELLIGENT DINOSAUR
FEATURES:	LARGE BRAIN, PARTIALLY OPPOSABLE THUMBS, SICKLE-SHAPED TOE CLAW, LARGE EYES
DIET:	LIZARDS, SNAKES, SMALL MAMMALS AND OTHER SMALL CREATURES

pointing upwards when running or walking. Its arms had a bird-like wrist joint that allowed them to fold in and back, rather like a bird folds its wings.

Hunting

Troodon had large eyes that would have enabled it to see well in the dark. They were also slightly forward facing which have allowed it limited binocular vision.

Troodon had a large brain to body size ratio, strongly suggesting it was one of the most intelligent dinosaurs.

Troodon had partially opposable thumbs, which would have helped it grasp branches and other objects more firmly. The opposable thumb was vital in human evolution as it allowed us to manipulate tools.

Troodon probably hunted at dusk or twilight when its night vision would give it an advantage. Troodon would have hunted small mammals and lizards and perhaps baby dinosaurs.

MEGA FACTS

- One of the first dinosaurs found in North America.

- Troodon may have supplemented its diet with plants, making it an omnivore.

- Fossilised Troodon nests have been found, suggesting that Troodon brooded over its eggs rather like hens.

- Had they not become extinct, dinosaurs like Troodon with their opposable thumbs and large brains might have developed to become intelligent creatures. In the 1980s, palaeontologist Dale Russell worked with artist Ron Sequin to produce a model of an upright dinosaur called Dinosauroid to show what such a creature could have looked like.

- Troody is a robotic Troodon built at MIT, to simulate how these creatures walked.

MEGALOSAURUS

Huge bipedal

M E A T E A T E R S

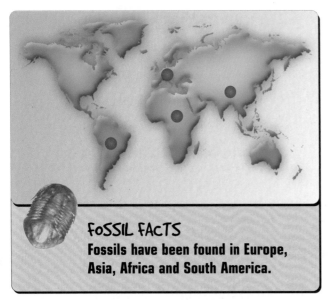

FOSSIL FACTS
Fossils have been found in Europe, Asia, Africa and South America.

Megalosaurus means 'great lizard'. It was named in 1824 and was the first dinosaur to be given a scientific name.

Appearance

No complete skeleton has yet been discovered so we cannot be 100% certain of what it looked like.

Megalosaurus had a big head, and its curved teeth had saw edges well suited to eating meat. Its jaws were very powerful. It had small eyes with bony knobs over the top of them and its head was held up by a strong, short neck.

This carnivore grew to a length of 30 ft, a height of 12 ft. It was bipedal. It had a long tail to help balance out its heavy head.

Its back legs were much longer than its arms. The arms had hands that could have been used for grasping. The legs ended in four-toed feet (one toe was reversed, like all therapod dinosaurs). Both fingers and toes had strong, sharp claws.

Diet

Megalosaurus was a powerful hunter, and could attack even the largest prey. It would have hunted plant-eating

Dinosaur Data

PRONUNCIATION:	**MEG**-UH-LOW-**SAWR**-US
SUBORDER:	THERAPODA
FAMILY:	MEGALOSAURIDAE
DESCRIPTION:	LARGE BIPEDAL CARNIVORE
FEATURES:	POWERFUL JAWS, BULKY BODY, LARGE HEAD
DIET:	OTHER DINOSAURS